My Journal

Date Today: 4/30/22

Today I'm Grateful for:

1) ...... My cat ....
2) ...... Moved 2.5 ....
3) ...... My soccer Ball ....

Draw, Write, Stick - Today's Best Bit!

Today I Feel: (draw Your Emoji!)

Date Today:..................

Today I'm Grateful for:

1)...

2)...

3)...

Draw, Write, Stick - Today's Best Bit!

Today I Feel: ◯ (draw Your Emoji!)

Date Today:................

Today I'm Grateful for:

1)..

2)..

3)..

Draw, Write, Stick - Today's Best Bit!

Today I Feel: (draw Your Emoji!)

Date Today:................

Today I'm Grateful for:

1)...

2)...

3)...

Draw, Write, Stick - Today's Best Bit!

Today I Feel: ⭕ (draw Your Emoji!)

Date Today:................

Today I'm Grateful for:

1)..

2)..

3)..

Draw, Write, Stick - Today's Best Bit!

Today I Feel:  (draw Your Emoji!)

Date Today:................

Today I'm Grateful for:

1)..

2)..

3)..

Draw, Write, Stick - Today's Best Bit!

Today I Feel: (draw Your Emoji!)

Date Today:...................

Today I'm Grateful for:

1)...

2)...

3)...

Draw, Write, Stick - Today's Best Bit!

Today I Feel: (draw your Emoji!)

Top Achievements This Week

....

....

....

....

This Week - I Want To Let Go Of:

☆ ☆ ☆ ☆ ☆ ☆

Draw, Write, Stick - Best Of The Week!

Free thought page... Write anything that comes into your mind - without boundaries!

WEEKLY GOALS

GOALS FOR MYSELF

M	T	W	TH	F
○	○	○	○	○
○	○	○	○	○
○	○	○	○	○

GOALS FOR SCHOOL/COLLEGE/UNI

M	T	W	TH	F
○	○	○	○	○
○	○	○	○	○
○	○	○	○	○

FRIENDSHIP/FAMILY GOALS

M	T	W	TH	F
○	○	○	○	○
○	○	○	○	○
○	○	○	○	○

Date Today:................

Today I'm Grateful for:

1)...

2)...

3)...

Draw, Write, Stick - Today's Best Bit!

Today I Feel: (draw Your Emoji!)

Date Today:.................

Today I'm Grateful for:

1)...

2)...

3)...

Draw, Write, Stick - Today's Best Bit!

Today I Feel: (draw Your Emoji!)

Date Today:...............

Today I'm Grateful for:

1)...

2)...

3)...

Draw, Write, Stick - Today's Best Bit!

Today I Feel: (draw Your Emoji!)

Date Today:.................

Today I'm Grateful for:

1)...

2)...

3)...

Draw, Write, Stick - Today's Best Bit!

Today I Feel: (draw Your Emoji!)

Date Today:..................

Today I'm Grateful for:

1)...

2)...

3)...

Draw, Write, Stick - Today's Best Bit!

Today I Feel: (⃝) (draw Your Emoji!)

Date Today:................

Today I'm Grateful for:

1)...

2)...

3)...

Draw, Write, Stick - Today's Best Bit!

Today I Feel: (draw Your Emoji!)

Date Today:................

Today I'm Grateful for:

1)...

2)...

3)...

Draw, Write, Stick - Today's Best Bit!

Today I Feel: ⬤ (draw Your Emoji!)

Top Achievements This Week

....

....

....

....

This Week - I Want To Let Go Of:

☆ ☆ ☆ ☆ ☆ ☆

Draw, Write, Stick - Best Of The Week!

Free thought page... Write anything that
comes into your mind - without boundaries!

WEEKLY GOALS

GOALS FOR MYSELF

M	T	W	TH	F
●	●	●	●	●
●	●	●	●	●
●	●	●	●	●

GOALS FOR SCHOOL/COLLEGE/UNI

M	T	W	TH	F
●	●	●	●	●
●	●	●	●	●
●	●	●	●	●

FRIENDSHIP/FAMILY GOALS

M	T	W	TH	F
●	●	●	●	●
●	●	●	●	●
●	●	●	●	●

Date Today:..................

Today I'm Grateful for:

1).......................................

2).......................................

3).......................................

Draw, Write, Stick - Today's Best Bit!

Today I Feel: (draw Your Emoji!)

Date Today:................

Today I'm Grateful for:

1)..

2)..

3)..

Draw, Write, Stick - Today's Best Bit!

Today I Feel: (draw Your Emoji!)

Date Today:..................

Today I'm Grateful for:

1)...

2)...

3)...

Draw, Write, Stick - Today's Best Bit!

Today I Feel: (draw Your Emoji!)

Date Today:.................

Today I'm Grateful for:

1)...

2)...

3)...

Draw, Write, Stick - Today's Best Bit!

Today I Feel: ( ) (draw Your Emoji!)

Date Today:..................

Today I'm Grateful for:

1)...

2)...

3)...

Draw, Write, Stick - Today's Best Bit!

Today I Feel: (draw Your Emoji!)

Date Today:................

Today I'm Grateful for:

1)...

2)...

3)...

Draw, Write, Stick - Today's Best Bit!

Today I Feel: (draw Your Emoji!)

Date Today:..............

Today I'm Grateful for:

1)...

2)...

3)...

Draw, Write, Stick - Today's Best Bit!

Today I Feel: ⃝ (draw Your Emoji!)

Top Achievements This Week

....

....

....

....

This Week - I Want To Let Go Of:

Draw, Write, Stick - Best Of The Week!

Free thought page... Write anything that
comes into your mind - without boundaries!

WEEKLY GOALS

GOALS FOR MYSELF

	M	T	W	TH	F
	○	○	○	○	○
	○	○	○	○	○
	○	○	○	○	○

GOALS FOR SCHOOL/COLLEGE/UNI

	M	T	W	TH	F
	○	○	○	○	○
	○	○	○	○	○
	○	○	○	○	○

FRIENDSHIP/FAMILY GOALS

	M	T	W	TH	F
	○	○	○	○	○
	○	○	○	○	○
	○	○	○	○	○

Date Today:................

Today I'm Grateful for:

1)...
2)...
3)...

Draw, Write, Stick - Today's Best Bit!

Today I Feel: (draw Your Emoji!)

Date Today:................

Today I'm Grateful for:

1)...

2)...

3)...

Draw, Write, Stick - Today's Best Bit!

Today I Feel: (draw Your Emoji!)

Date Today:................

Today I'm Grateful for:

1)...

2)...

3)...

Draw, Write, Stick - Today's Best Bit!

Today I Feel: ◯ (draw Your Emoji!)

Date Today:...............

Today I'm Grateful for:

1)..

2)..

3)..

Draw, Write, Stick - Today's Best Bit!

Today I Feel: (draw Your Emoji!)

Date Today:..................

Today I'm Grateful for:

1)...

2)...

3)...

Draw, Write, Stick - Today's Best Bit!

Today I Feel: (draw Your Emoji!)

Date Today:................

Today I'm Grateful for:

1)...

2)...

3)...

Draw, Write, Stick - Today's Best Bit!

Today I Feel: ( ) (draw your Emoji!)

Date Today:.................

Today I'm Grateful for:

1)...

2)...

3)...

Draw, Write, Stick - Today's Best Bit!

Today I Feel: (draw Your Emoji!)

Top Achievements This Week

....

....

....

....

This Week - I Want To Let Go Of:

☆ ☆ ☆ ☆ ☆ ☆

Draw, Write, Stick - Best Of The Week!

Free thought page... Write anything that comes into your mind - without boundaries!

WEEKLY GOALS

GOALS FOR MYSELF

M   T   W   TH   F

GOALS FOR SCHOOL/COLLEGE/UNI

M   T   W   TH   F

FRIENDSHIP/FAMILY GOALS

M   T   W   TH   F

Date Today:................

Today I'm Grateful for:

1)......................................

2)......................................

3)......................................

Draw, Write, Stick - Today's Best Bit!

Today I Feel: (draw Your Emoji!)

Date Today:...............

Today I'm Grateful for:

1)..

2)..

3)..

Draw, Write, Stick - Today's Best Bit!

Today I Feel: (draw Your Emoji!)

Date Today:.................

Today I'm Grateful for:

1)...

2)...

3)...

Draw, Write, Stick - Today's Best Bit!

Today I Feel: (draw Your Emoji!)

Date Today:.................

Today I'm Grateful for:

1)...

2)...

3)...

Draw, Write, Stick - Today's Best Bit!

Today I Feel: (draw Your Emoji!)

Date Today:.................

Today I'm Grateful for:

1)...

2)...

3)...

Draw, Write, Stick - Today's Best Bit!

Today I Feel: ⬭ (draw Your Emoji!)

Date Today:...............

Today I'm Grateful for:

1)...

2)...

3)...

Draw, Write, Stick - Today's Best Bit!

Today I Feel: ( ) (draw Your Emoji!)

Date Today:................

Today I'm Grateful for:

1)...

2)...

3)...

Draw, Write, Stick - Today's Best Bit!

Today I Feel: ◯ (draw Your Emoji!)

Top Achievements This Week

....

....

....

....

This Week - I Want To Let Go Of:

☆ ☆ ☆ ☆ ☆ ☆

Draw, Write, Stick - Best Of The Week!

Free thought page... Write anything that
comes into your mind - without boundaries!

WEEKLY GOALS

GOALS FOR MYSELF

M T W TH F

○ ○ ○ ○ ○

○ ○ ○ ○ ○

○ ○ ○ ○ ○

GOALS FOR SCHOOL/COLLEGE/UNI

M T W TH F

○ ○ ○ ○ ○

○ ○ ○ ○ ○

○ ○ ○ ○ ○

FRIENDSHIP/FAMILY GOALS

M T W TH F

○ ○ ○ ○ ○

○ ○ ○ ○ ○

○ ○ ○ ○ ○

Date Today:................

Today I'm Grateful for:

1)...

2)...

3)...

Draw, Write, Stick - Today's Best Bit!

Today I Feel: ( ) (draw Your Emoji!)

Date Today:.................

Today I'm Grateful for:

1)...

2)...

3)...

Draw, Write, Stick - Today's Best Bit!

Today I Feel: ⭕ (draw Your Emoji!)

Date Today:...................

Today I'm Grateful for:

1)..

2)..

3)..

Draw, Write, Stick - Today's Best Bit!

Today I Feel: (draw Your Emoji!)

Date Today:...................

Today I'm Grateful for:

1)...

2)...

3)...

Draw, Write, Stick - Today's Best Bit!

Today I Feel: ◯ (draw Your Emoji!)

Date Today:................

Today I'm Grateful for:

1)...

2)...

3)...

Draw, Write, Stick - Today's Best Bit!

Today I Feel: (draw Your Emoji!)

Date Today:................

Today I'm Grateful for:

1)...

2)...

3)...

Draw, Write, Stick - Today's Best Bit!

Today I Feel: ( ) (draw Your Emoji!)

Date Today:...............

Today I'm Grateful for:

1)...

2)...

3)...

Draw, Write, Stick - Today's Best Bit!

Today I Feel: ( ) (draw Your Emoji!)

Top Achievements This Week

....

....

....

....

This Week - I Want To Let Go Of:

☆ ☆ ☆ ☆ ☆ ☆

Draw, Write, Stick - Best Of The Week!

Free thought page... Write anything that
comes into your mind - without boundaries!

WEEKLY GOALS

GOALS FOR MYSELF

M	T	W	TH	F
○	○	○	○	○
○	○	○	○	○
○	○	○	○	○

GOALS FOR SCHOOL/COLLEGE/UNI

M	T	W	TH	F
○	○	○	○	○
○	○	○	○	○
○	○	○	○	○

FRIENDSHIP/FAMILY GOALS

M	T	W	TH	F
○	○	○	○	○
○	○	○	○	○
○	○	○	○	○

Date Today:...............

Today I'm Grateful for:

1)..

2)..

3)..

Draw, Write, Stick - Today's Best Bit!

Today I Feel: (draw Your Emoji!)

Date Today:................

Today I'm Grateful for:

1)..

2)..

3)..

Draw, Write, Stick - Today's Best Bit!

Today I Feel: (draw Your Emoji!)

Date Today:................

Today I'm Grateful for:

1)...

2)...

3)...

Draw, Write, Stick - Today's Best Bit!

Today I Feel: (draw Your Emoji!)

Date Today:................

Today I'm Grateful for:

1)..

2)..

3)..

Draw, Write, Stick - Today's Best Bit!

Today I Feel: ⬭ (draw Your Emoji!)

Date Today:.................

Today I'm Grateful for:

1)...
2)...
3)...

Draw, Write, Stick - Today's Best Bit!

Today I Feel: (draw Your Emoji!)

Date Today:...................

Today I'm Grateful for:

1)...

2)...

3)...

Draw, Write, Stick - Today's Best Bit!

Today I Feel: (draw Your Emoji!)

Date Today:................

Today I'm Grateful for:

1)..

2)..

3)..

Draw, Write, Stick - Today's Best Bit!

Today I Feel: ( )   (draw Your Emoji!)

Top Achievements This Week

....

....

....

....

This Week - I Want To Let Go Of:

☆ ☆ ☆ ☆ ☆ ☆

Draw, Write, Stick - Best Of The Week!

Free thought page... Write anything that comes into your mind - without boundaries!

WEEKLY GOALS

GOALS FOR MYSELF

	M	T	W	TH	F
	○	○	○	○	○
	○	○	○	○	○
	○	○	○	○	○

GOALS FOR SCHOOL/COLLEGE/UNI

	M	T	W	TH	F
	○	○	○	○	○
	○	○	○	○	○
	○	○	○	○	○

FRIENDSHIP/FAMILY GOALS

	M	T	W	TH	F
	○	○	○	○	○
	○	○	○	○	○
	○	○	○	○	○

Date Today:................

Today I'm Grateful for:

1)...

2)...

3)...

Draw, Write, Stick - Today's Best Bit!

Today I Feel: (draw Your Emoji!)

Date Today:................

Today I'm Grateful for:

1)..

2)..

3)..

Draw, Write, Stick - Today's Best Bit!

Today I Feel: (draw Your Emoji!)

Date Today:...............

Today I'm Grateful for:

1)...

2)...

3)...

Draw, Write, Stick - Today's Best Bit!

Today I Feel: (draw Your Emoji!)

Date Today:................

Today I'm Grateful for:

1)..

2)..

3)..

Draw, Write, Stick - Today's Best Bit!

Today I Feel: (draw Your Emoji!)

Date Today:..................

Today I'm Grateful for:

1)...

2)...

3)...

Draw, Write, Stick - Today's Best Bit!

Today I Feel: (draw Your Emoji!)

Date Today:................

Today I'm Grateful for:

1)...

2)...

3)...

Draw, Write, Stick - Today's Best Bit!

Today I Feel: ( ) (draw Your Emoji!)

Date Today:................

Today I'm Grateful for:

1)..

2)..

3)..

Draw, Write, Stick - Today's Best Bit!

Today I Feel: (draw Your Emoji!)

Top Achievements This Week

....

....

....

....

This Week - I Want To Let Go Of:

☆ ☆ ☆ ☆ ☆ ☆

Draw, Write, Stick - Best Of The Week!

Free thought page... Write anything that comes into your mind - without boundaries!

WEEKLY GOALS

GOALS FOR MYSELF

M	T	W	TH	F

GOALS FOR SCHOOL/COLLEGE/UNI

M	T	W	TH	F

FRIENDSHIP/FAMILY GOALS

M	T	W	TH	F

Date Today:...............

Today I'm Grateful for:

1)...

2)...

3)...

Draw, Write, Stick - Today's Best Bit!

Today I Feel: ◯ (draw Your Emoji!)

Date Today:..............

Today I'm Grateful for:

1)..
2)..
3)..

Draw, Write, Stick - Today's Best Bit!

Today I Feel: (draw Your Emoji!)

Date Today:..................

Today I'm Grateful for:

1)...

2)...

3)...

Draw, Write, Stick - Today's Best Bit!

Today I Feel: ◯ (draw Your Emoji!)

Date Today:................

Today I'm Grateful for:

1)...

2)...

3)...

Draw, Write, Stick - Today's Best Bit!

Today I Feel: (   ) (draw Your Emoji!)

Date Today:................

Today I'm Grateful for:

1)...

2)...

3)...

Draw, Write, Stick - Today's Best Bit!

Today I Feel: (draw Your Emoji!)

Date Today:................

Today I'm Grateful for:

1)...

2)...

3)...

Draw, Write, Stick - Today's Best Bit!

Today I Feel: (draw Your Emoji!)

Date Today:..............

Today I'm Grateful for:

1)..

2)..

3)..

Draw, Write, Stick - Today's Best Bit!

Today I Feel: (draw Your Emoji!)

Top Achievements This Week

....
....
....
....

This Week - I Want To Let Go Of:

Draw, Write, Stick - Best Of The Week!

Free thought page... Write anything that comes into your mind - without boundaries!

WEEKLY GOALS

GOALS FOR MYSELF

M	T	W	TH	F
○	○	○	○	○
○	○	○	○	○
○	○	○	○	○

GOALS FOR SCHOOL/COLLEGE/UNI

M	T	W	TH	F
○	○	○	○	○
○	○	○	○	○
○	○	○	○	○

FRIENDSHIP/FAMILY GOALS

M	T	W	TH	F
○	○	○	○	○
○	○	○	○	○
○	○	○	○	○

Date Today:................

Today I'm Grateful for:

1)...

2)...

3)...

Draw, Write, Stick - Today's Best Bit!

Today I Feel: (draw Your Emoji!)

Date Today:..................

Today I'm Grateful for:

1)..

2)..

3)..

Draw, Write, Stick - Today's Best Bit!

Today I Feel: (draw Your Emoji!)

Date Today:................

Today I'm Grateful for:

1)...

2)...

3)...

Draw, Write, Stick - Today's Best Bit!

Today I Feel: ⭕ (draw Your Emoji!)

Date Today:................

Today I'm Grateful for:

1)...

2)...

3)...

Draw, Write, Stick - Today's Best Bit!

Today I Feel: ( ) (draw Your Emoji!)

Date Today:................

Today I'm Grateful for:

1)...
2)...
3)...

Draw, Write, Stick - Today's Best Bit!

Today I Feel: ◯ (draw Your Emoji!)

Date Today:...............

Today I'm Grateful for:

1)...

2)...

3)...

Draw, Write, Stick - Today's Best Bit!

Today I Feel: (draw Your Emoji!)

Date Today:................

Today I'm Grateful for:

1)...

2)...

3)...

Draw, Write, Stick - Today's Best Bit!

Today I Feel: (draw Your Emoji!)

Top Achievements This Week

....

....

....

....

This Week - I Want To Let Go Of:

☆ ☆ ☆ ☆ ☆ ☆

Draw, Write, Stick - Best Of The Week!

Free thought page... Write anything that comes into your mind - without boundaries!

WEEKLY GOALS

GOALS FOR MYSELF

M	T	W	TH	F

GOALS FOR SCHOOL/COLLEGE/UNI

M	T	W	TH	F

FRIENDSHIP/FAMILY GOALS

M	T	W	TH	F

Date Today:.................

Today I'm Grateful for:

1)...

2)...

3)...

Draw, Write, Stick - Today's Best Bit!

Today I Feel: ◯ (draw Your Emoji!)

Date Today:....................

Today I'm Grateful for:

1)...

2)...

3)...

Draw, Write, Stick - Today's Best Bit!

Today I Feel: ( ) (draw Your Emoji!)

Date Today:...............

Today I'm Grateful for:

1).......................................

2).......................................

3).......................................

Draw, Write, Stick - Today's Best Bit!

Today I Feel: (draw Your Emoji!)

Date Today:................

Today I'm Grateful for:

1)..

2)..

3)..

Draw, Write, Stick - Today's Best Bit!

Today I Feel: ⬭ (draw Your Emoji!)

Date Today:..................

Today I'm Grateful for:

1)..

2)..

3)..

Draw, Write, Stick - Today's Best Bit!

Today I Feel: ( ) (draw Your Emoji!)

Date Today:................

Today I'm Grateful for:

1)...

2)...

3)...

Draw, Write, Stick - Today's Best Bit!

Today I Feel: (draw Your Emoji!)

Date Today:................

Today I'm Grateful for:

1)..

2)..

3)..

Draw, Write, Stick - Today's Best Bit!

Today I Feel: (draw Your Emoji!)

Top Achievements This Week

....

....

....

....

This Week - I Want To Let Go Of:

☆ ☆ ☆ ☆ ☆ ☆

Draw, Write, Stick - Best Of The Week!

Free thought page... Write anything that comes into your mind - without boundaries!

WEEKLY GOALS

GOALS FOR MYSELF

M	T	W	TH	F
○	○	○	○	○
○	○	○	○	○
○	○	○	○	○

GOALS FOR SCHOOL/COLLEGE/UNI

M	T	W	TH	F
○	○	○	○	○
○	○	○	○	○
○	○	○	○	○

FRIENDSHIP/FAMILY GOALS

M	T	W	TH	F
○	○	○	○	○
○	○	○	○	○
○	○	○	○	○

Date Today:....................

Today I'm Grateful for:

1)...

2)...

3)...

Draw, Write, Stick - Today's Best Bit!

Today I Feel: (draw Your Emoji!)

Date Today:..................

Today I'm Grateful for:

1)...
2)...
3)...

Draw, Write, Stick - Today's Best Bit!

Today I Feel: (draw Your Emoji!)

Date Today:.................

Today I'm Grateful for:

1)..

2)..

3)..

Draw, Write, Stick - Today's Best Bit!

Today I Feel:  (draw Your Emoji!)

Date Today:.................

Today I'm Grateful for:

1)...

2)...

3)...

Draw, Write, Stick - Today's Best Bit!

Today I Feel: (draw Your Emoji!)

Date Today:...............

Today I'm Grateful for:

1)...

2)...

3)...

Draw, Write, Stick - Today's Best Bit!

Today I Feel: ( ) (draw Your Emoji!)

Date Today:.................

Today I'm Grateful for:

1)...

2)...

3)...

Draw, Write, Stick - Today's Best Bit!

Today I Feel: ( ) (draw Your Emoji!)

Date Today:..................

Today I'm Grateful for:

1)...

2)...

3)...

Draw, Write, Stick - Today's Best Bit!

Today I Feel: ( ) (draw Your Emoji!)

Top Achievements This Week

....

....

....

....

This Week - I Want To Let Go Of:

Draw, Write, Stick - Best Of The Week!

Free thought page... Write anything that comes into your mind - without boundaries!